About the Marine Sanctuaries Conservation Series

The National Oceanic and Atmospheric Administration's National Ocean Service (NOS) administers the Office of National Marine Sanctuaries (ONMS). Its mission is to identify, designate, protect and manage the ecological, recreational, research, educational, historical, and aesthetic resources and qualities of nationally significant coastal and marine areas. The existing marine sanctuaries differ widely in their natural and historical resources and include nearshore and open ocean areas ranging in size from less than one to over 5,000 square miles. Protected habitats include rocky coasts, kelp forests, coral reefs, sea grass beds, estuarine habitats, hard and soft bottom habitats, segments of whale migration routes, and shipwrecks.

Because of considerable differences in settings, resources, and threats, each marine sanctuary has a tailored management plan. Conservation, education, research, monitoring and enforcement programs vary accordingly. The integration of these programs is fundamental to marine protected area management. The Marine Sanctuaries Conservation Series reflects and supports this integration by providing a forum for publication and discussion of the complex issues currently facing the sanctuary system. Topics of published reports vary substantially and may include descriptions of educational programs, discussions on resource management issues, and results of scientific research and monitoring projects. The series facilitates integration of natural sciences, socioeconomic and cultural sciences, education, and policy development to accomplish the diverse needs of NOAA's resource protection mandate.

Reconciling Ecosystem-Based Management and Focal Resource Conservation in the Papahānaumokuākea Marine National Monument

John N. Kittinger[1], Derek J. Skillings[2], Kimo K. Carvalho[3], Lora L.N. Reeve[4], Melanie Hutchinson[5], Katherine Cullison[6], Janna Shackeroff[7], Malia Chow[8], Judith Lemus[9]

1. Department of Geography, University of Hawai'i at Mānoa, National Science Foundation Graduate Fellow, Integrated Graduate Education, Research and Training (IGERT) Program in Ecology, Conservation and Pathogen Biology, 445 Saunders Hall, 2424 Maile Way, Honolulu, HI 96822, Email: jkittinger@gmail.com
2. Hawai'i Institute of Marine Biology, University of Hawai'i, P.O. Box 1346, Kāne'ohe, HI, 96744, Email: derek.skillings@gmail.com
3. Papahānaumokuākea Marine National Monument, 6600 Kalaniana'ole Hwy, #300, Honolulu, HI 96825, Email: Kimo.Carvalho@noaa.gov
4. W.S. Richardson School of Law and Department of Zoology, University of Hawai'i at Mānoa, 2538 McCarthy Mall, Edmondson 152, Honolulu, HI 96822, Email: lreeve@hawaii.edu
5. Hawai'i Institute of Marine Biology, University of Hawai'i, Post Office Box 1346, Kāne'ohe, Hawaii 96744, Email: melanier@hawaii.edu
6. Department of Botany, University of Hawai'i at Mānoa, 3190 Maile Way, Honolulu, HI 96822, Email: kate1@hawaii.edu
7. At time of report preparation: Papahānaumokuākea Marine National Monument, 6600 Kalaniana'ole Hwy, #300, Honolulu, HI 96825; Current: NOAA's Coral Reef Conservation Program, 1305 East West Hwy, Silver Spring, MD 20910, Email: Janna.Shackeroff@noaa.gov
8. Papahānaumokuākea Marine National Monument, 6600 Kalaniana'ole Hwy, #300, Honolulu, HI 96825, Email: Malia.Chow@noaa.gov
9. Hawai'i Institute of Marine Biology, University of Hawai'i at Mānoa, P.O. Box 1346, Kāne'ohe, HI, 96744, Email: jlemus@hawaii.edu

U.S. Department of Commerce
Gary Locke, Secretary

National Oceanic and Atmospheric Administration
Jane Lubchenco, Ph.D.
Under Secretary of Commerce for Oceans and Atmosphere

National Ocean Service
John H. Dunnigan, Assistant Administrator

Silver Spring, Maryland
December 2009

Office of National Marine Sanctuaries
Daniel J. Basta, Director

DISCLAIMER

Report content does not necessarily reflect the views and policies of the Office of National Marine Sanctuaries or the National Oceanic and Atmospheric Administration, nor does the mention of trade names or commercial products constitute endorsement or recommendation for use.

REPORT AVAILABILITY

Electronic copies of this report may be downloaded from the Office of National Marine Sanctuaries web site at www.sanctuaries.nos.noaa.gov. Hard copies may be available from the following address:

National Oceanic and Atmospheric Administration
Office of National Marine Sanctuaries
SSMC4, N/ORM62
1305 East-West Highway
Silver Spring, MD 20910

COVER

Photos are the property of Papahānaumokuākea Marine National Monument

SUGGESTED CITATION

Kittinger, J.N., D.J. Skillings, K.K. Carvalho, L.L.N. Reeve, M. Hutchinson, K. Cullison, J. Shackeroff, M. Chow, J. Lemus. 2010. Reconciling Ecosystem-Based Management and Focal Resource Conservation in the Papahānaumokuākea Marine National Monument. Marine Sanctuaries Conservation Series ONMS-09-04. U.S. Department of Commerce, National Oceanic and Atmospheric Administration, Office of National Marine Sanctuaries, Silver Spring, MD. 36pp.

CONTACT

John N. (Jack) Kittinger
Department of Geography
University of Hawai'i at Mānoa
445 Saunders, 2424 Maile Way
Honolulu, Hawai'i 96822, USA
Telephone: (808) 956-8465
Fax: (808) 956-3512
Email: jkittinger@gmail.com

Table of Contents

List of Figures and Tables

Executive Summary

In May 2008, the National Center for Ecological Analysis and Synthesis (NCEAS) conducted a "Distributed Graduate Seminar" bringing graduate students and faculty from seven universities, Office of National Marine Sanctuary (ONMS) staff, and other interested parties to examine Marine Protected Areas (MPAs) as effective tools for Ecosystem-Based Management (EBM). Students, faculty, ONMS staff, and guest lecturers used NCEAS informatics tools to connect with each other via an online course website, video conferencing, and a chat bulletin board to discuss how ecosystem processes within MPAs can allow resource managers to manage MPAs as integral components of the ecosystems in which they reside. As a course product, students at each university were required to produce a case study of a MPA within their respective regions. Students addressed how their MPA can effectively implement EBM within its boundaries, contribute to broader EBM efforts within their region, and how their MPAs can meet local management objectives and simultaneously contribute to broader regional objectives. Students also discussed the legal and jurisdictional barriers and opportunities for EBM efforts at local and regional scales.

Currently throughout the Pacific region, there is an increasing trend in protecting larger-scale marine areas, which includes managing many different stakeholder groups and multiple biological, socio-economic, ecological, and cultural resources. Additionally, with the establishment of new U.S. Marine National Monuments, co-managing agencies are mandated to work with each other to manage multiple resources via an EBM approach. This case study uses the Papahānaumokuākea Marine National Monument (monument) as an example of how co-managers currently implement EBM into large-scale MPA management. Through working with monument staff and discussing the challenges and obstacles of managing this large-scale MPA, University of Hawaii at Mānoa (UH-Mānoa) graduate students proposed a new planning and management approach to better integrate EBM and conservation of focal resources in monument via a prioritization process that identifies the biological, cultural, and social resources through a stakeholder process that can aid protected area management.

Following the Graduate Seminar, UH-Mānoa graduate students discussed their case study with monument managers. Results were positive in nature. The group encouraged the monument's three co-managing agencies to strategically implement EBM into future programs and activities using innovative EBM tools, such as the one described below. Additionally, graduate students from all participating universities, including UH-Mānoa, were able to come together at a working group meeting in Santa Barbara, California in April 2009 to exchange perspectives, experiences, and knowledge to develop scholarly products based on collective student work during their seminars. This information will help the ONMS effectively implement EBM management approaches within their boundaries and contribute to broader EBM efforts in the regions in which they occur.

Key Words

Marine Spatial Planning, Ecosystem Based Management, Marine Protected Areas, Protected Resources, Focal Resources, Papahānaumokuākea Marine National Monument, Northwestern Hawaiian Islands, Ecosystem Vulnerability

1.0   Introduction

In the marine environment, protected areas have become one of the principal tools for conserving ecosystems. An increasing recognition of the threats to marine ecosystems has led to a focus on establishing protections at regional biogeographic scales, which has led to the establishment of MPA networks and large, regional-scale MPAs. Regional protections have been predicated on the need to match institutional management on the scales relevant to ecosystem processes (Folke et al. 2007, Galaz et al. 2007), and the need to protect larger percentages and representative habitat types within the marine environment for conservation efficacy and risk management (Bohnsack et al. 2002, Sherman 1991). Large-scale MPAs face different challenges in governance and management than small-scale or community-based MPAs, including multiple agency management, complex and overlapping legal mandates and authorities, expanded and more diverse stakeholder groups, and various resource use interests (Kittinger et al. 2009). This increased socio-political complexity presents many challenges to institutions responsible for the planning and management of large-scale MPAs (Day 2008, Day 2002, Hughes et al. 2007, Kittinger et al. 2009, Olsson et al. 2008).

Principal among these challenges is reconciling the somewhat conflicting mandates of holistic ecosystem protection and conservation of focal resources (Noss et al. 2002). Focal resources, defined here, include resources such as species or sites that are protected by legal statute and require special management. In contrast, ecosystem-based management requires consideration of the broader ecosystem, including the elements, processes, and functions that comprise a functional ecosystem together with human influences on ecosystem condition (Arkema et al. 2006, Browman et al. 2004, Crowder and Norse 2008, Olsson et al. 2008). EBM is now becoming the accepted approach in environmental management (Leslie and McLeod 2007, Olsson et al. 2008), but few operative frameworks have been advanced to address the statutory mandates that require agencies to specially manage key focal resources. Such conflicts in management are typically addressed in the planning and spatial management of activities ("use") within protected areas, which is typically addressed in the iterative updating of management plans (Kittinger et al. 2009, Salafsky et al. 2001).

This paper presents a proposed methodology for the integration of ecosystem-based management and conservation of focal resources in protected areas via a prioritization process for resource conservation. The proposed methodology relies upon a prioritization of resources, determination of resource vulnerability, and integration into a spatial conservation planning tool. First, the origins and scientific basis for ecosystem-based marine management are reviewed. Next, the concept of ecosystem vulnerability as a method for integrating ecosystem and focal resource protections is proposed. A comprehensive planning process and three-step method are then described for quantifying vulnerability for use in marine spatial planning (MSP) tools. Finally, specific applications to management of protected areas are articulated.

1.1 Ecosystem-Based Marine Management

The integration of the principles and concepts of natural resource management, conservation biology, and ecosystem sustainability is now referred to as an "ecosystem" or "ecosystem-based" approach, and is a primary focus in conventional marine resource management (Arkema et al.

2006, Grumbine 1994, Gunderson et al. 1995, Leslie and McLeod 2007, Ruckelshaus et al. 2008). In the marine realm, EBM emerged within the development of the integrative discipline of marine conservation biology, which included concepts and principles of protected area design and management. Its first general texts (Norse and Crowder 2005a, Sobel and Dahlgren 2004) and compendium of articles (Ecological Applications 2003) appeared more than two decades after the publication of the first conservation biology text, which drew from and focused on terrestrial biodiversity (Soule and Wilcox 1980). This time lag has been attributed to the greater amenability of the latter to research and conservation (Norse and Crowder 2005b).

Ecosystem-based management (EBM) has evolved from initial establishment of its scientific basis, to articulation of guiding principles and concepts, and finally to operational implementation by management institutions (McLeod and Leslie 2009). The scientific basis and general principles of ecosystem based management have been established (Browman et al. 2004, Christensen et al. 1996, Ecosystem Principles Advisory Panel 1999), and general guiding principles have been proposed. In marine conservation, general principles include recognition of the importance of spatial and temporal scale, the interconnectivity of ecosystems, engagement with stakeholders, adaptive management, and consideration of society as an intrinsic component of ecological systems (Brodziak and Link 2002, Crowder and Norse 2008, Leslie and McLeod 2007, Link 2002, Ruckelshaus et al. 2008). Though EBM principles have yet to be integrated into most governance mechanisms and statutes in the US (Parenteau et al. 2008), agencies involved in ecosystem management have begun to implement EBM concepts into 'soft law' policy and practice. In the literature, operative approaches to marine EBM are now being proposed (Arkema et al. 2006, Barnes and McFadden 2008, Gaichas 2008); additionally, international agencies have begun to explore the adoption of EBM principles into management actions (FAO 2003, Garcia et al. 2003).

The ecosystem-based approach for natural resource management planning on federal lands became policy in the U.S. over a decade ago (Council on Environmental Quality et al. 1995), and articulation of its scientific basis has been proposed specifically to address the problem of sustaining marine fisheries (Ecological Applications 1998, NRC 1999). The policy mechanisms for applying the ecosystem approach in the U.S. primarily include the iterative updating and implementing of resource and habitat management plans for federal lands of conservation significance (including submerged lands), fishery management plans (Kittinger 2008), and protected area management plans (Parenteau et al. 2008).

1.2   Integrative Approaches to Ecosystem Management

The development of integrative, transdisciplinary theory and research has been spurred by a general recognition that traditional disciplinary approaches are inadequate to confront problems of society and environment (Berkes et al. 2003, Hirsch Hadorn et al. 2008). Integrative research efforts have applied concepts from varying fields of social and natural sciences and other disciplines to environmental management (e.g., Gunderson et al. 1995). In particular, the application of concepts of health derived from the biomedical sciences has emerged in the context of ecosystem management (Costanza et al. 1992). The ecosystem health concept has been utilized in integrated assessment and protection of conjoint social and ecological systems through explicit recognition and characterization of social-ecological linkages (Costanza and

Mageau 1999, Epstein et al. 1994, Lebel 2003, Millennium Ecosystem Assessment 2005). Within the context of ecosystem health and management, the concept of vulnerability has arisen as an effective assessment method for characterizing and prioritizing the linkages between social and ecological systems, particularly in the context of environmental services relied upon by human societies (Adger 2006).

In the marine realm, ecological vulnerability first arose in the context of planning for and responding to natural hazards, including potential oil spills (Gundlach and Hayes 1978, Michel et al. 1978). Further development of the vulnerability concept has been promulgated in the literature of systematic conservation planning (Margules and Pressey 2000, Wilson et al. 2005). The primary purpose in determining ecological vulnerability is to prioritize conservation actions for specific resources, which often takes place in the process of spatial planning for protected areas. A synthesis of the vulnerability concept as applied to ecological systems is presented below. In the following section, a method is introduced for prioritizing conservation of resources in protected area planning and management of the Papahānaumokuākea Marine National Monument (monument).

2.0 Reconciling Conflicting Mandates in the Papahānaumokuākea Marine National Monument

2.1   Papahānaumokuākea Marine National Monument Ecosystem Protections

The Papahānaumokuākea Marine National Monument (monument) comprises the Northwestern Hawaiian Islands (NWHI) – a chain of islands, atolls, and shoals spanning approximately 2,000 kilometers beyond the Main Hawaiian Islands (MHI), both of which make up the Hawaiian Archipelago in the Pacific Ocean (Figure 1). Legal protections for the natural resources in the monument date to 1909 (Executive Order 199A) when President Theodore Roosevelt established what is now known as the Hawaiian Islands National Wildlife Refuge (Executive Order 1019, Presidential Proclamation 2416). The unique values, global significance, and ecological vulnerability of the NWHI were again recognized by the federal government in Executive Order 13178 (2000) (Executive Order 13178), and finalized by Executive Order 13196 (2001) (Executive Order 13196), establishing the NWHI Coral Reef Ecosystem Reserve (Reserve) and initiating a process to designate a National Marine Sanctuary (Sanctuary). Additionally, the State of Hawai'i recognized the significance of the NWHI by establishing the Northwestern Hawaiian Islands State Marine Refuge (DLNR 2005). The biological and cultural significance of the monument has been documented by expeditions to the NWHI (Grigg et al. 2008), multiple research symposia (DiNardo and Parrish 2006, Grigg and Pfund 1980, Grigg and Tanoue 1984), and its recent nomination for recognition as a UNESCO World Heritage Site (State of Hawaii et al. 2009).

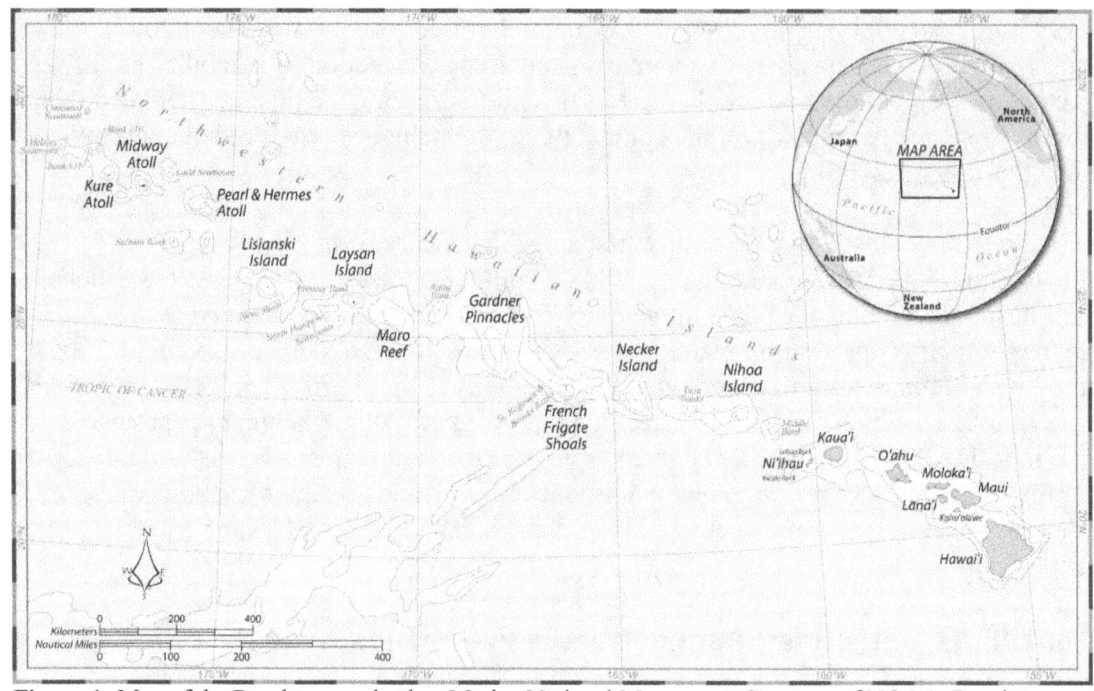

Figure 1: Map of the Papahānaumokuākea Marine National Monument. Courtesy of NOAA, Papahānaumokuākea Marine National Monument Office

On June 15, 2006, President Bush issued Presidential Proclamation 8031 (Proclamation) (Department of Commerce et al. 2006, Presidential Proclamation 8031), creating the NWHI Marine National Monument under the Antiquities Act of 1906 (American Antiquities Act of 1906). Later renamed the Papahānaumokuākea Marine National Monument (monument) (Presidential Proclamation 8112), the Proclamation recognizes the global biological and socio-cultural significance of the NWHI and the need for strong environmental protection. The proclamation preserved the existing management responsibilities of two federal agencies and the State of Hawaii (Table 1), as well as pre-existing ecosystem protections. The National Oceanic and Atmospheric Administration (NOAA), U.S. Fish and Wildlife Service (USFWS), and the State of Hawai'i have been designated as monument "Co-Trustees," with the mandate to work cooperatively in the management of the monument. Specific management protocols were outlined for implementation in an interagency memorandum of agreement (Memorandum of Agreement 2006). A suite of policies and regulations exist associated with the Co-Trustee agencies, along with applicable state and Federal laws, (e.g. Endangered Species Act, Marine Mammal Protection Act, Migratory Bird Treaty Act), to which management of the protected area is to conform.

Resource	Example	Category
Coral	Poritidea, Pocilloporidea, Acroporidea, deepwater 'precious' corals	Habitat, species
Algae	Chlorophyta, Rhodophyta, Phaeophyta, Cyanophyta, *Halimeda*, coralline	Habitat, species
Misc. Benthic Shallow Water Invertebrates	Mollusca, Porifea, Anthropoda	Species
Lobster	Palinuridae, Scyllaridae	Species
Reef fish	Apex predators, herbivores,	Species
Bottomfish	Lutjanidae, Serranidae, Carangidae, Lethrinidae	Species
Pelagic Marine Life	Scombroidae, Carcharhinidae,	Species
Reptiles	*Caretta carretta, Chelonia mydas, Lepidochelys olivacae, Dermochelys coriacea, Eretmochelys imbricata*	Species
Land Birds	Passerines (3), Laysan Duck	Species
Shore Birds	*Pluvialis fulva, Numenius tahitiensis, Tringa incana, Arenaria interpres*	Species
Sea Birds	Albatross, shearwaters, petrel, terns, boobys	Species
Marine Mammals	*Monachus schauinslandi*, Cetaceans (20+)	Species
Terrestrial Invertebrates	Arachnida, Insecta, Chilopoda, Gastropoda	Species
Terrestrial Plants	*Achyranthes atollensis, Phyloostegia variabilis, Pritchardia* spp.	Habitat, species
Endangered and Threatened Species	Marine mammals, marine turtles, terrestrial birds, seabirds, terrestrial plants	Species
Native Hawaiian Ancestral Sites		Socio-Cultural
Native Hawaiian Ceremonial Foundations	Ceremonial terraces and platform foundations (Nihoa, Mokumanamana)	Socio-Cultural
Maritime Heritage	Ship wrecks, military WWII sites	Socio-Cultural

Table 1: Resources of the Northwestern Hawaiian Islands, as identified by the Papahānaumokuākea Marine National Monument Management Plan (MMP) (USFWS et al. 2008). 'Misc benthic shallow water invertebrates' is substituted for 'crustaceans,' because crustaceans include lobsters, which are disaggregated in the MMP.

2.2 *Reconciling Conflicting Resource Management Mandates in the Monument*

The monument is the largest protected area in the United States, and one of the largest MPAs in the world. Like many protected areas, the monument contains focal resources (e.g. the endangered Hawaiian monk seal, Native Hawaiian cultural sites) requiring special management actions, as well as the mandate to manage the protected area via an ecosystem approach. For managing institutions, the legal mandates that require special protection of focal resources can result in significant investment of agency resources to a disproportionately small element of the ecosystem. For example, in the monument a suite of management actions have been directed toward conservation of the endangered monk seal. The significant investment of management effort in the Hawaiian monk seal is a consequence of the monk seal's protected status under the Endangered Species Act, which prescribes specific actions to which managing agencies are

13

required to conform. Conservation strategies employed by managing agencies have included exhaustive monitoring programs, relocation of males to reduce deleterious male-mobbing behaviors, catch-and-release programs to revitalize malnourished pups, and the removal of Galapagos sharks that prey on juvenile pups. The focus on saving the endangered monk seal takes place within a broader effort by co-trustees to manage the entire ecosystem of the monument. From an ecosystem function perspective, the monk seal is a critical component of the functional group of apex predators in the monument. The diversity of functional groups has been recognized as a key feature of maintaining ecological resilience (Bengtsson et al. 2003, Hughes et al. 2003, Nyström and Folke 2001, Nyström et al. 2000), although there are emerging arguments against this assertion (*e.g.* Bellwood et al. 2003). Loss of functional group diversity and intact populations can result in phase shifts to undesired states, as has been observed in the Caribbean region (Box 1) (Nyström et al. 2000). For the Hawaiian monk seal, the critical question from the whole ecosystem perspective then becomes at what population level does the monk seal become ecologically extinct, and how would the resilience of the monument ecosystem be impacted if the monk seal was to go extinct? From a broader ecosystem perspective, the goals should be to preserve the diversity of functional groups in the monument in order to maximize ecological resilience and prevent shifts to undesirable ecosystem states that can be caused by human and environmental disturbances acting synergistically. Notably, both approaches require an understanding of the historical baseline of ecological states, population densities and species' roles in the ecosystem, as well as disturbance regimes (human and natural) in managed ecosystem.

Box 1. Phase shift in Caribbean coral reefs (adapted from Nyström et al. 2000)

In the past three decades, coral reef ecosystems in the Caribbean region have undergone a dramatic transition from hard coral to fleshy algae dominance. The factors behind this change include a combination of natural (hurricanes and disease) and anthropogenic (overfishing and nutrient increase) disturbances acting in synergy. Due to overfishing, by the late 1960-70s fish biomass had been heavily reduced, and the reefs around Jamaica were extensively damaged. Because large predatory fish were continuously overfished, herbivorous fish became the new target species. The loss of herbivorous fish resulted in the competitive release of the sea urchin *Diadema antillarium* which increased significantly in abundance and became the keystone herbivore. In 1981, a hurricane killed or damaged most of the branching coral species, resulting in new open substratum becoming available for colonization by fast growing algae. Despite high levels of nutrients, algal densities were kept low by the efficient grazing *Diadema*, and coral recolonization took place. However, in 1982 and 1983, the sea urchin population suffered from a species-specific pathogen that reduced the population by 99% in some areas. It is speculated that the high host density of *Diadema* enabled efficient transmission of the pathogen, to which *Diadema* exhibited an extremely low resistance. Additionally, the loss of host diversity in the coral reef ecosystem probably reduced the natural capacity of the ecosystem to dilute the pathogen and therefore buffer populations from epidemic disease. Because all major grazers were then low in numbers, they were not able to prevent the establishment of algae, resulting in a dramatic change in the abundance ratio between coral and benthic algae. Brown fleshy algae became overwhelmingly abundant and prevented coral larvae settlement. This case demonstrates how the loss of diversity within the functional group of herbivores resulted in reduced resilience of the coral reef ecosystem. A disturbance that could previously be buffered by a diverse functional group of herbivores, became the trigger that caused an ecosystem with reduced resilience to shift from a coral-dominated state to one dominated by algae. The extent to which this phase shift is irreversible is still unclear.

The above example (Box 1) illustrates the difference in management approaches to the conservation of focal resources versus broader, ecosystem-based management. To reconcile these approaches, we propose a prioritization process for resource conservation (Figure 2). This integrative planning and management process includes three primary steps:

1) Resource identification and prioritization through a participatory stakeholder process;
2) Resource vulnerability determinations through an expert interview method, and;
3) Integration of vulnerability determination and prioritization of resources into a conservation priority index that can be integrated into marine spatial planning tools to aid in ecosystem planning and management.

The first step is a value-driven process whereby stakeholders identify the resources and attributes of the protected area and subsequently prioritize the resources for management actions. The second step is an expert opinion survey method which assigns vulnerability determinations to resources. A third and final step is the integration of stakeholder resource prioritization data (established in step 1) with vulnerability determinations (step 2), which results in a resource-specific conservation prioritization index. Conservation priority indices for specific resources can be then be integrated via geospatial information tools for ecosystem-based analysis and decision-making by managing agencies. Each step in this process is described in more detail below.

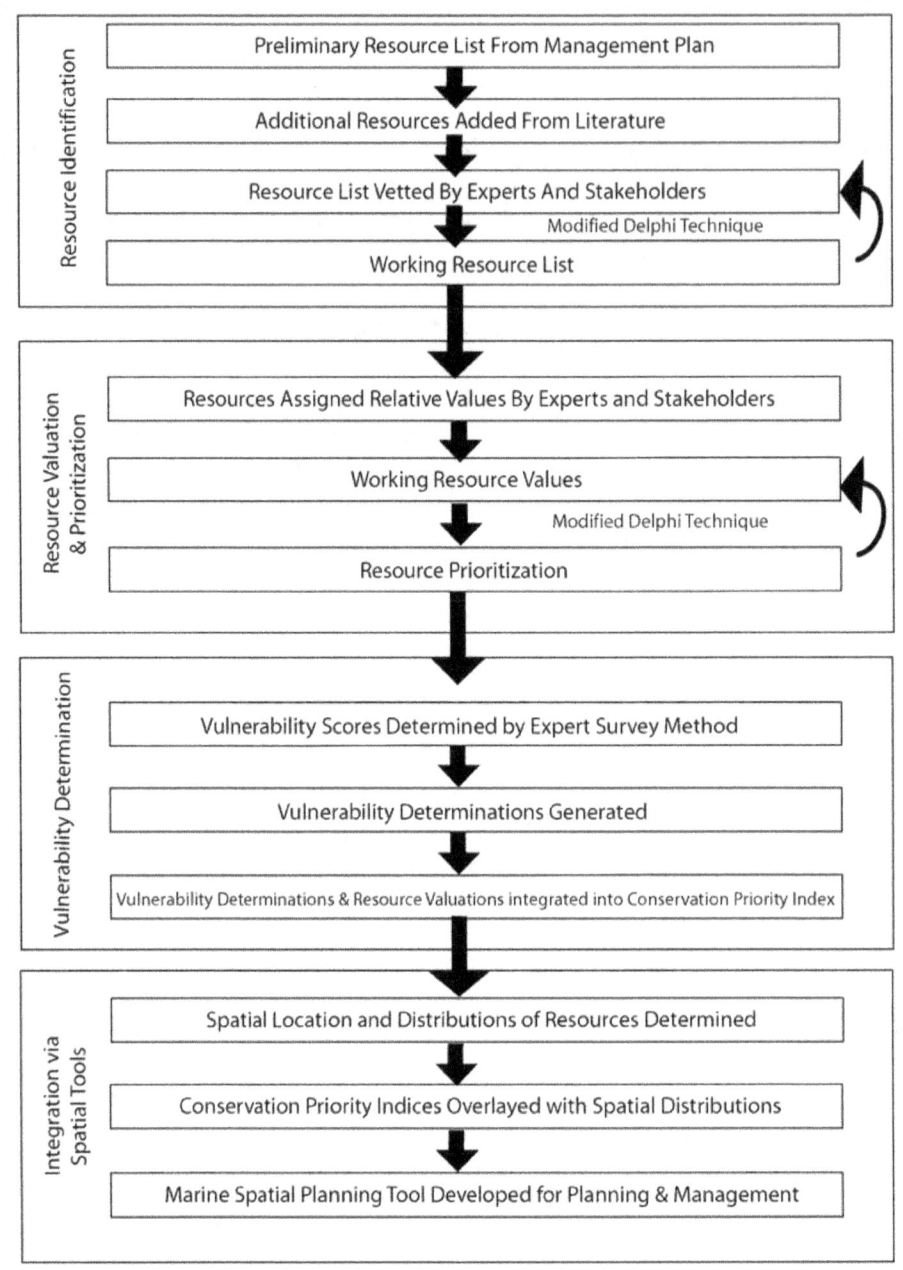

Figure 2: Flow chart showing the progressive steps in a conservation planning framework for resource identification, prioritization, vulnerability determination, and integration via spatial planning tools.

2.3   *Step 1: Resource Identification*

In protected areas, resources have variably been defined as habitats, areas, species, processes, or artifacts that have societal value (Zacharias and Gregr 2005). In an ecosystem context, the term 'resource' does not necessarily imply resources expressly targeted for extraction by human uses, but also includes elements and processes critical to ecosystem function, such as habitat, interspecies connections, and processes. Additionally, based on the EBM thinking which emphasizes the interconnectedness of economic, political, social, and ecological dimensions, 'resources' also include place-specific features that hold particular cultural or aesthetic value.

A critical first step in the conservation planning process is to build a consensus on what resources in the protected area are valued by different stakeholders. This includes identification of the resources that are valued in the managed ecosystem by stakeholders and constituents. Subsequently, resources are ranked or prioritized for management actions based on their perceived value to stakeholders. Identifying and prioritizing resources should optimally be accomplished in a systematic, participatory stakeholder process (Berghöfer et al. 2008, Noss et al. 2002) that attempts to reach a consensus or agreement amongst stakeholders. As part of this process, managing agencies may generate a preliminary resource list as a basic framework to facilitate discussions by stakeholders. Subsequently, stakeholder discussions and results from expert opinion surveys may be integrated to form a more comprehensive resource list.

2.3.1 *Establishing a Preliminary Resource List*

A preliminary resource list was derived from the Monument Management Plan (MMP) (USFWS et al. 2008) (Table 1 in section 2.1). Specific resources were initially identified in the MMP section entitled 'Status and Condition of the Natural Resources and Environmental and Anthropogenic Stressors;' this list includes all resources given a subheading in this section of the MMP. Subsequently each subsection of the action plans within the MMP as well as the Environmental Assessment was reviewed and considered while developing the Preliminary Resource List. We modified an approach from (Zacharias and Gregr 2005), where resources were grouped and placed into categories, including: Habitat, Species, Socio-Cultural, and Ecosystem Processes (Table 1 in section 2.1). These categories may be subject to change based on expert opinion surveys and data gathered by stakeholders during the valuation process in order to develop a more comprehensive list.

The preliminary resource list was subsequently expanded by adding resources identified in a survey of related literature in academic journals (Table 2). The following key words were used to search academic journals available through online databases from the University of Hawai'i at Mānoa: MPA, EBM, Protected Resources, Focal Resources, PMNM, NWHI, Ecosystem Threats, Ecosystem Vulnerability, and Ecosystem Risk. Databases were searched by graduate students at the University of Hawai'i at Mānoa. The resultant list represents an expanded array of resources identified as integral to ecosystem function as well as socio-cultural value (Hiddink et al. 2007, Hiscock and Tyler-Walters 2006, Noss et al. 2002, Selkoe et al. 2008, Zacharias and Gregr 2005). Notably, this resource list includes not only biological elements (e.g., habitats, species), but also biotic and abiotic processes which are critical attributes of ecosystem function. Finally, a preliminary list of socio-cultural resources is included, with an express caveat: it is expected that engagement with Native Hawaiian stakeholders in the process would substantially expand and further define the resources identified here as having cultural significance in the NWHI.

Resource	Code	Source	Description
Ecozones & Habitats	E1		Pelagic
	E2	MMP	Deep Reef
	E3	MMP	Outer Reef
	E4	MMP	Inner Reef
	E5		Pavement
	E6		Sand / Mud
	E7	MMP	Algal Beds
	E8		Sandy Beach
	E9		Rocky Intertidal
	E10		Interior Terrestrial
	E11		Unclassified Habitat (Other)
	H1		Seamounts
	H2		Lagoons
	H3		Tidal Passages
	H4		Spawning Sites
	H5		Areas of High Biodiversity (Spp. Richness, Diversity)
Biological Resources	B1	MMP	Threatened, Endangered and Protected Species
	B2		Endemic Species
	B3	MMP	Biogenic Reefs
	B4	MMP	Seabirds, Shorebirds
	B5	MMP	Marine Mammals
	B6		Migratory Species
	B7	MMP	Benthic Shallow Water Invertebrates
	B8	MMP	Crustaceans
	B9	MMP	Reef Fish
	B10	MMP	Bottom Fish
	B11	MMP	Pelagic Marine Life
	B12	MMP	Reptiles
	B13		Long-lived, Low Reproductive Species
Socio-Cultural Resources	SCR1	MMP	Native Hawaiian Ancestral Sites
	SCR2	MMP	Native Hawaiian Ceremonial Foundations
	SCR3	MMP	Maritime Heritage Sites
Processes	P1		Seasonal Spawning/Reproduction Events
	P2		Pacific Decadal Oscillation, Geostrophic Fronts
	P3		Ecological-Evolutionary Connectivity

Table 2: Example of an ecosystem-based resource list for the monument. A species or group of species was categorized as 'Habitat' if it provides critical habitat for other species (e.g. biogenic corals). The 'Species' category was assigned to species or groups of species that are considered an important resource, either for extractive or aesthetic values, or if the species plays a critical role in ecosystem function. The 'Socio-Cultural' category

represents resources that have special significance in terms of military or seafaring history or Native Hawaiian culture. Lastly, 'Processes' were identified for specific abiotic and biotic events that have broad-reaching effects across the NWHI coral reef ecosystem. MMP indicates this resource was identified in the Monument Management Plan (USFWS et al. 2008).

2.3.2 Stakeholder Mechanisms for Resource Valuation and Prioritization

Once generated, the preliminary resource list can then be evaluated by a group of experts and stakeholders in order for them to add, alter, and prioritize the resources. Ideally, stakeholders and experts should reach a consensus, but consensus building amongst competing interest groups may be difficult. Indeed, different stakeholder groups hold different definitions of what constitutes a resource as well as different valuations for different resources. Inherent in these differing resource valuations are the varying motives, interests, worldviews and belief systems that comprise stakeholder groups in protected areas and elsewhere.

Within the disciplines of decision science and conservation planning there are many methods that are commonly used for consensus building amongst interested parties. We will highlight a technique referred to as the modified Delphi Method, an accepted method in the field of conservation biology and social sciences utilized to reach consensus among competing interest groups (Crance 1987, Linstone and Turoff 2002). We selected the Delphi Method because the technique allows participants to remain anonymous to each other and thus minimizes bias and conflict. Alternative methods include focus groups, public comment and meetings, or facilitated workshops with stakeholder groups. The Delphi Method is an iterative systematic survey technique that is used to build towards a consensus or agreement among pre-determined participants. Survey questions are distributed amongst participants who are anonymous to each other. Answers are consolidated and redistributed back to the participants by the investigators along with the original question list and/or additional questions. Survey participants are then allowed to change their answers based on previous answers and justifications by others in the group. Because participants are anonymous to each other, this method is able to circumvent problems that may arise from face-to-face and group interactions. The iterative survey process allows competing participants to convince each other and change their answers without "losing face." This structured process of collecting and disseminating all available data continues until consensus, stasis, or a predetermined number of rounds has been reached. For MPA management and planning, a modified Delphi Method should include: 1) reaching consensus on a final resource list; and, 2) determination of quantitative prioritization (valuation metrics) for individual resources.

A quantitative valuation metric specific to each resource must be derived from the survey process. This quantitative metric would be a function of individual scores from survey participants rating the importance of individual resources according to biological, ecological, cultural, legal, and economic importance. These ranked values are incorporated with vulnerability determinations to arrive at what can be viewed as a conservation priority index for each resource in the protected area (Figure 3).

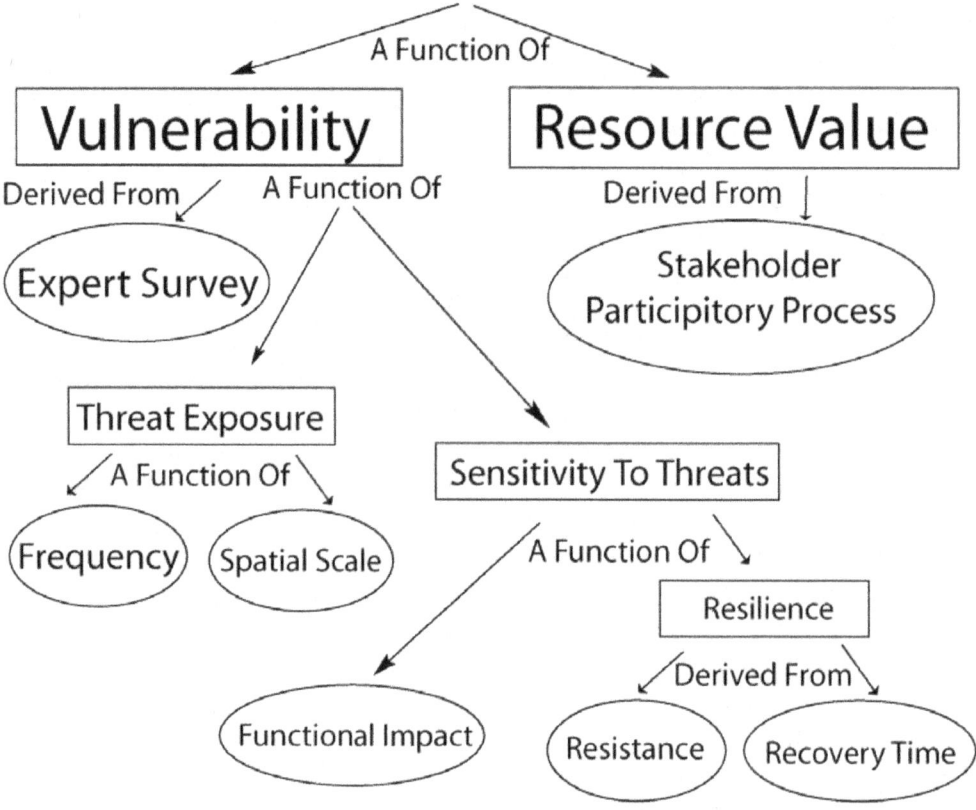

Figure 3: Conceptualization of a resource conservation prioritization index, which is a function of vulnerability and resource value (prioritization ranking). Vulnerability is a function of risk and sensitivity. Risk is a probabilistic function of the spatial and temporal scale of anthropogenic threats. Resource sensitivity is a function of the functional impact of a stressor to a resource, as well as the resilience of a resource, defined as its resistance to a stressor, and recovery time after the occurrence of a stressor.

The results obtained from using the Delphi Method are only as robust as the expertise of the group of individuals chosen to participate in the process as well as the questions that are used in the survey. If participants are not an adequate representation of their chosen field of expertise, or not enough participants are included to capture the field, then the results may not be an accurate representation and therefore not repeatable. It is critical that survey participants include stakeholders and experts with knowledge of the protected area. We define stakeholders as any group that has a direct or indirect stake in the decision-making process. Stakeholders include individuals, groups, or institutions that can be affected by the results of the decision-making process. Experts include individuals with academic training in a topic germane to the ecosystem, those with tenured knowledge of the ecosystem, indigenous cultural experts, or others with similar qualifications (Grimble and Wellard 1997, Pomeroy and Douvere 2008).

For the monument, stakeholders and experts include, but are not limited to: Native Hawaiian cultural practitioners, managers from the Co-Trustee agencies, academic and research scientists (biophysical and social scientists), extractive resource users (recreational and commercial), members of non-governmental organizations, and members of the public. These expert groups comprise the stakeholders identified as critical to inclusion in the planning process, based on the identified metrics of power, legitimacy, and urgency (Mitchell et al. 1997, Scott and Lane 2000). It is important to note that experts and stakeholders tend to be viewed as distinct groups, though in some cases they may overlap. Finally, it is critical that qualified social scientists or professional facilitators are engaged in the design, execution, and analysis of the survey process.

2.4   *Step 2: Resource Vulnerability Determinations*

Vulnerability has arisen as a key concept for prioritizing management strategies, particularly in conservation planning, and various definitions and methods for determining vulnerability have been proposed (Wilson et al. 2005, Wilson et al. 2006). As used here, vulnerability is defined as a function of the *sensitivity* of a resource to a stressor or disturbance, combined with the *risk* of the stressor or disturbance occurring (Figure 3). Sensitivity is defined as the degree to which resources respond to stresses, where stresses are deviations of environmental conditions beyond the expected range (Zacharias and Gregr 2005). Risk is a probability function for the occurrence of a specific event, such as a stressor or disturbance (Saaty 1987). Vulnerability is therefore the probability that a resource will be exposed to a stressor to which it is sensitive (FAO 2007, Halpern et al. 2007, Hiddink et al. 2007, Zacharias and Gregr 2005).

Various methods have been proposed for determining quantitative measures of vulnerability, but most studies have focused on a single species approach (e.g. Garthe and Huppop 2004). The three primary methods proposed in the literature include: 1) ranking data obtained in a literature review, 2) expert opinion survey, and 3) site-based algorithms. A repeatable, quantitative survey method is the most appropriate and tractable method by which to assess, from an ecosystem level, environmental vulnerability (Halpern et al. 2007). The methods presented in Halpern et al. (2007) and applied to identifying and ranking threats in the NWHI by Selkoe et al. (2008b) can be used in a comprehensive survey of expert opinions to determine quantitatively the vulnerability of resources in the monument and bring focal and ecosystem-level resources into a common framework. As defined above, experts include academically-trained or similarly qualified individuals with deep knowledge and experience, including those intimately familiar with the protected area.

Halpern et al. (2007) present five criteria for determining vulnerability, which can be grouped under the two primary concepts underlying vulnerability, that of risk and sensitivity (Figure 3). These metrics include the (1) spatial scale and (2) temporal frequency of a stressor, which together comprise the probabilistic function of risk. For sensitivity, metrics include the (3) functional impact (number of trophic levels affected), (4) the resistance to impact, and, (5) the recovery time required to return to a pre-impact conditions.

Resource sensitivity therefore includes considerations of both the likelihood that a resource will experience substantial alteration from short-term or chronic disturbance, and the length of time required to recover to its prior state after a disturbance (FAO 2007, Halpern et al. 2007, Zacharias and Gregr 2005). The most sensitive resources are therefore those that are both easily disturbed and are slow to recover, or may never recover. Sensitive ecosystem features may be physically fragile, but some may be functionally fragile even if physically robust. Therefore, a resource is defined as sensitive to a threat or stressor if it would be harmed, diminished, or altered due to the stressor or threat. A resource is vulnerable if it is likely that it would be exposed to a stressor in a frequency or duration that causes the stressor to affect it.

For individual resources, a quantitative determination of vulnerability requires identification of the stressors or threats to the resources in a protected area. For protected areas, the stressors of concern are direct anthropogenic stressors (e.g., marine debris, ship groundings), or indirect anthropogenic stressors, which are those stressors that have been exacerbated via human actions (e.g., sea level rise due to human-induced climate change). For the monument, the threats have been determined in previous work by (Selkoe et al. 2008b) and mapped spatially (Selkoe et al. 2008a).

2.5   *Step 3: Integration into Spatial Conservation Planning Applications*

A key benefit of the vulnerability concept is the prioritization of resources for conservation actions. In order for the vulnerability concept to be useful to managers and the decision-making process the vulnerability determinations and prioritization/valuation ranking must be mapped spatially. Using spatial mapping tools, areas that contain resources of special significance can be overlayed by layers of sensitivity and risk analyses. The result is a geospatial model of vulnerability. Spatial mapping also allows managers to integrate disparate information sets into a matrix that can inform decision-makers on a time scale relevant to management. Integration of various datasets into a marine spatial planning process provides a mechanism for data from research and monitoring to be incorporated into the management of the ecosystem.

Several software applications exist for integrating data into geospatial systems for eco-regional conservation planning. A suite of site-based algorithms have been developed into software for conservation planning and configuration. Marxan is among the most sophisticated and appropriate for marine spatial planning, because it allows users to analyze and resolve multiple layers of data, including conservation targets (e.g. focal resources) and spatial management goals (e.g. 60% of spawning habitats protected) (Leslie et al. 2003, Possingham et al. 2000, Ball and Possingham 2000).

Marxan provides a mechanism to determine a hierarchical set of decision rules in spatial analyses. It assigns values to spatial planning units based on ecological and social criteria, which are then selected from among potential planning sites for the creation of a spatially cohesive reserve system that meets the goals set for protection of biodiversity or other conservation targets. It also includes tools for setting priorities, objectives, and budgets. Thus Marxan can be used for re-zoning considerations but also has an irreplaceability function which maps outputs and gives an indicative measure of the importance of individual planning units for meeting conservation objectives. Currently, researchers at The Ecology Centre and Centre for Applied Environmental Decision Analysis at the University of Queensland are developing new applications for Marxan to depict probabilistic information such as the probability of catastrophes occurring into the conservation planning process (http://www.uq.edu.au/MARXAN/index.html?page=77644&p=1.1.2.2).

The Marxan algorithm contains an objective function with which it runs all possible scenarios. In our proposed methodology, the objective function would be optimized for a vulnerability determination. To depict the vulnerability determinations using Marxan the planning region must be defined, in this case it will be the boundary of the monument. Next, conservation features are chosen that reflect regional ecology, availability of data, and relevance to desired planning objectives. The resource list shown in Table 1 (in section 2.1) summarizes the conservation features (and some of the subdivisions for the planning units) of monument. Data on resources (conservation feature) sensitivity and risk can then be manipulated to create spatial representations of vulnerability.

Information from the stakeholder resource identification and prioritization process (step 1) and expert surveys for vulnerability determinations (step 2) can be integrated with other spatial information through spatial mapping tools (e.g. GIS). Once a prioritized resource list is established (see Table 1 in section 2.1) each resource can be mapped spatially based on existing information on the distribution and spatial characterization of the managed ecosystem using Arcview, ArcGIS or other GIS software. Information on the risk of a stressor occurring can be mapped both spatially and by temporal frequency; e.g. for the NWHI, this information has been determined (Selkoe et al. 2008a, 2008b). The conservation priority index values for each resource , as determined by results of Steps 1-2 (sections 2.3-2.4), can be further integrated with biological and abiotic data available from research and monitoring activities.

The solutions or outputs from a Marxan analysis are a timely and useful means of incorporating large datasets with a huge area and complex questions. It allows for the integration of datasets generated in ongoing research and monitoring efforts. For the monument, large monitoring data sets exist, and research activities are consistently generating new data streams and information useful to management. Since the available information and the issues will constantly change, Marxan can be run many times with revised conservation targets to give up-to-date overlays of the most vulnerable areas within the monument. Spatial vulnerability determinations are also useful for more effective enforcement and monitoring of a reserve system (Leslie et al. 2003). Considering the large area of the monument, this would be of particular importance to identify areas that are critical areas to zone for special biodiversity protections, or monitor for violations.

3.0   Application to Planning and Management of the NWHI: Marine Spatial Planning

Various applications and tools that comprise marine spatial planning (MSP) approaches have been applied in marine ecosystem management. Ehler and Douvere (2007) define MSP as "analyzing and allocating parts of three-dimensional marine spaces to specific uses, to achieve ecological, economic, and social objectives that are usually specified through the political process." In MPAs, MSP focuses on a spatial approach to managing ocean-space, including zoning for multiple use, special ecosystem protections, surveillance, and other human uses (Crowder and Norse 2008, Douvere 2008, Douvere and Ehler 2008, Ehler and Douvere 2007). The adoption of spatial approaches is the result of an increased recognition, primarily among ecologists and resource managers, of the efficacy of spatial management in managing social-ecological complexity, including negativisms ("externalities") associated with common property regimes (Berkes et al. 2006, Crowder et al. 2006, Day 2002, Dietz et al. 2003, Lubchenco et al.

2003). Additionally, MSP is now recognized as a viable method for implementing ecosystem-based management (Crowder and Norse 2008, Friedlander et al. 2007, Ruckelshaus et al. 2008). We address two primary MSP approaches for our vulnerability determination process that can be used in planning and management of the NWHI, including zoning and surveillance.

3.1 *Zoning in the NWHI*

Currently, the NWHI has been spatially zoned into three areas: Special Preservation Areas (SPAs), Ecological Reserves, and the Midway Atoll Special Management Area. The purpose of this zonation is to protect sensitive habitats and preserve ecological services. The existing zonation scheme was arrived at by using bathymetric curves to delineate SPAs and areas outside of the existing bottom fishing areas were classified as Ecological Reserves. The current zoning system was based on a 'blanket' approach to set aside large areas, rather than a systematic, ecosystem-based approach recommended here.

The proposed methodology provides an ecosystem-based approach for integrating information into spatial management of the monument. Rather than being based on bathymetry alone, this methodology will allow for meaningful identification of vulnerable areas for relevant zoning schemes. Greater certainty will be provided because zones will be delineated by physical habitat, species distribution, physical and biological processes, or locations of high human value (e.g. native Hawaiian and marine archeology sites). Under this type of zoning scheme, human activities within the monument could be evaluated based on informed criteria and spatial vulnerability.

Additionally, this work will build on existing research efforts in the NWHI. In particular, the existing characterization of anthropogenic threats (Selkoe et al. 2008b) has been mapped spatially (Selkoe et al. 2008a), identifying areas that are most susceptible to threats. The spatial characterization of the vulnerability of resources in the NWHI, in conjunction with threat mapping (Selkoe et al. 2008a), monitoring data, and spatial data on cumulative impacts of human activities (Halpern et al. 2008) will allow managers to effectively plan and manage the NWHI protected ecosystem. Such planning and management can more effectively address permitted or allowed activities in the monument. These activities include commercial vessel traffic, recreation, siting of cables and pipelines, anchoring, military activities, and prioritization of research needs for management. For example, dedicated commercial shipping lanes and ocean cables could be relocated to areas away from identified vulnerable areas, and within a bank scale, specific anchoring locations could be identified. While the US military is not restricted in any way within the monument, the identification of vulnerable areas could be used by the military to voluntarily conduct exercises in less-vulnerable areas.

3.2 *Surveillance*

Effective MSP also requires enforcement of existing statutes and regulations, in effect, monitoring illegal activities through surveillance. Human activities in the monument that are targets for surveillance include three user categories:

1) permitted users that violate the conditions of their permits (e.g. bottomfish vessels fishing in restricted areas),

2) non-permitted legal activities (e.g. vessels engaged in passive transit through the NWHI), and,

3) non-permitted users engaged in illegal activities (e.g. illegal foreign-flagged vessels).

The threats associated with these different users may impact monument resources at different scales, and are part of surveillance and threat assessment being conducted by the monument.

Enforcement concerns in monument center on ensuring compliance with monument regulations. Currently, surveillance of the monument includes monthly flights by the United States Coast Guard (USCG). During these flyovers a crew can survey a swath of approximately 50 nm given the altitude and variety of tools (USCG 2008). While monthly flights could conceivably cover the entire width of the monument, the planes are instructed to avoid areas with large concentrations of birds in order to minimize impacts, therefore, flights must offset the islands, potentially leaving important ecological areas essentially unmonitored. This current surveillance scheme attempts to cover the maximum area without specific focus areas. USCG personnel have expressed a certain degree of frustration with the current scheme, stating that "we could do a much better job if we knew where to look" (USCG 2008).

Identification of vulnerable areas in the monument would allow surveillance flights to focus specifically on these areas. For instance, if illegal fishing vessels were thought to be exploiting monument resources at specific banks or specific habitats within banks (vulnerable areas as identified by this methodology) flights could be adjusted to target those areas. Identification of vulnerable areas will also allow monument managers to use other resources for surveillance. The primary permitted activity in the monument is research. Informing researchers working in zones deemed vulnerable (see above) about the zone-specific threats adds 'eyes and ears' with communication abilities to the managers. Coastal and land-based vulnerable areas could be monitored via remote surveillance cameras and off-shore areas could be monitored via satellite.

Scientific research has and continues to play a critical role in defining the biological value of the resources and ecosystems of the monument (DiNardo and Parrish 2006, Grigg and Pfund 1980, Grigg and Tanoue 1984). A prioritization scheme can help to direct resources and monitoring to fill particular management needs, particularly on those areas deemed vulnerable and high conservation priorities.[1] For surveillance, informing researchers working in zones deemed priority areas about the threats specific to that area adds surveillance capacity to the NWHI.

4.0   Conclusions

---

[1] The analysis presented here supports, unequivocally, the importance of research, including biophysical, socio-cultural, indigenous, and other, as integral to informing effective management of the NWHI. As such, it is believed by the authors that the spatial prioritization of resources in the NWHI would help identify critical areas where research needs can inform management. The authors do not support the restriction of research critical to understanding resources in the NWHI.

This paper proposes a comprehensive planning process for ecosystem-based management in protected areas. The process includes multiple steps, and engages with stakeholders, experts, and managing institutions in a participatory process. The proposed framework integrates concepts from social and biophysical sciences and thus espouses a transdisciplinary approach to these issues in ecosystem planning and management. Ideally, the proposed process would be conducted on a recurring timescale to inform the iterative updating of the management plan for the marine protected area. This would add an adaptive management approach to the management plan review process. Significantly, this proposed method would help to resolve the conflicting mandates of focal resource management and an ecosystem-based approach to management. It does so by prioritizing resources through various surveying methods, and integrating the resultant information into geospatial planning platforms that can become dynamic tools for use by managers.

5. 0 Acknowledgements

This manuscript was prepared as a case study for a distributed course on the role of marine protected areas in ecosystem-based management, coordinated jointly by the National Center for Ecological Analysis and Synthesis, the Hawaii Institute for Marine Biology, and the Papahānaumokuākea Marine National Monument. The authors thank Kim Selkoe and Joseph O'Malley for their help in preparing this manuscript and their comments on early drafts, which greatly improved the quality of the work. The authors also thank the natural resource managers, professors, and experts who participated in the class.

6.0 References

Adger, W. N. 2006. Vulnerability. Global Environmental Change 16:268-281.

American Antiquities Act of 1906. 16 U.S.C. 431-433.

Arkema, K. K., S. C. Abramson, and B. M. Dewsbury. 2006. Marine ecosystem-based management: from characterization to implementation. Frontiers in Ecology and the Environment 4:525-532.

Barnes, C., and K. W. McFadden. 2008. Marine ecosystem approaches to management: challenges and lessons in the United States. Marine Policy 32:387-392.

Bellwood, D. R., A. S. Hoey, and J. H. Choat. 2003. Limited functional redundancy in high diversity systems: resilience and ecosystem function on coral reefs. Ecology Letters 6:281-285.

Bengtsson, J., P. Angelstam, T. Elmqvist, U. Emanuelsson, C. Folke, M. Ihse, F. Moberg, and M. Nyström. 2003. Reserves, resilience and dynamic landscapes. Ambio 32:389-396.

Berghöfer, A., H. Wittmer, and F. Rauschmayer. 2008. Stakeholder participation in ecosystem-based approaches to fisheries management: A synthesis from European research projects. Marine Policy 32:243-253.

Berkes, F., J. Colding, and C. Folke 2003. Navigating social-ecological systems: building resilience for complexity and change. Cambridge University Press, Cambridge.

Berkes, F., T. P. Hughes, R. S. Steneck, J. A. Wilson, D. R. Bellwood, B. Crona, C. Folke, L. H. Gunderson, H. M. Leslie, J. Norberg, M. Nystrom, P. Olsson, H. Osterblom, M. Scheffer, and B. Worm. 2006. Globalization, roving bandits, and marine resources. Science 311:1557-1558.

Bohnsack, J. A., B. Causey, M. P. Crosby, R. B. Griffis, M. A. Hixon, T. F. Hourigan, K. H. Koltes, J. E. Maragos, A. Simons, and J. T. Tilmant. 2002. A rationale for minimum 20-30% no-take protection. Pages 615-619. Proceedings of the Ninth International Coral Reef Symposium, Bali, 23-27 October 2000.

Brodziak, J., and J. Link. 2002. Ecosystem-based fishery management: What is it and how can we do it? Bulletin of Marine Science 70:589-611.

Browman, H. I., K. I. Stergiou, P. M. Cury, R. Hilborn, S. Jennings, H. K. Lotze, P. M. Mace, S. Murawski, D. Pauly, M. Sissenwine, K. I. Stergiou, and D. Zeller. 2004. Perspectives on ecosystem-based approaches to the management of marine resources. Marine Ecology Progress Series 274:269-303.

Christensen, N. L., A. M. Bartuska, J. H. Brown, S. Carpenter, C. D'Antonio, R. Francis, J. F. Franklin, J. A. MacMahon, R. F. Noss, D. J. Parsons, C. H. Peterson, M. G. Turner, and R. G. Woodmansee. 1996. The report of the ecological society of America committee on the scientific basis for ecosystem management. Ecological Applications 6:665-691.

Costanza, R., B. G. Norton, and B. D. Haskell, editors. 1992. Ecosystem health: New goals for environmental management. Island Press, Washington, DC.

Costanza, R., and M. Mageau. 1999. What is a healthy ecosystem? Aquatic Ecology 33:105-115.

Council on Environmental Quality, Department of Agriculture, Department of the Army, Department of Commerce, Department of Defense, Department of Energy, Department of Housing and Urban Development, Department of the Interior, Department of Justice, Department of Labor, Department of State, Department of Transportation, Environmental Protection Agency, and Office of Science and Technology Policy. 1995. Memorandum of understanding to foster the ecosystem approach. United States Department of Transportation, Federal Highway Administration, Office of Environment and Planning, Washington, DC.

Crance, J. H. 1987. Guidelines for using the Delphi technique to develop habitat suitability index curves. Biological Report No. 82 (10.134). National Ecology Center, Division of Wildlife and Contaminant Research, Fish and Wildlife Service, US Dept. of the Interior, Washington, DC.

Crowder, L., and E. Norse. 2008. Essential ecological insights for marine ecosystem-based management and marine spatial planning. Marine Policy 32:772-778.

Crowder, L. B., G. Osherenko, O. R. Young, S. Airamé, E. A. Norse, N. Baron, J. C. Day, F. Douvere, C. N. Ehler, B. S. Halpern, S. J. Langdon, K. L. McLeod, J. C. Ogden, R. E. Peach, A. A. Rosenberg, and J. A. Wilson. 2006. Resolving mismatches in U.S. ocean governance. Science 313:617-618.

Day, J. 2008. The need and practice of monitoring, evaluating and adapting marine planning and management--lessons from the Great Barrier Reef. Marine Policy 32:823-831.

Day, J. C. 2002. Zoning–lessons from the Great Barrier Reef Marine Park. Ocean and Coastal Management 45:139-156.

Department of Commerce, National Oceanic and Atmospheric Administration, Department of Interior, and Fish and Wildlife Service. 2006. Final Rule, Northwestern Hawaiian Islands Marine National Monument. 71 Fed. Reg. 51134, (Aug. 29, 2006), Washington, D.C.

Dietz, T., E. Ostrom, and P. C. Stern. 2003. The struggle to govern the commons. Science 302:1907-1912.

DiNardo, G. T., and F. A. Parrish. 2006. Northwestern Hawaiian Islands third scientific symposium, November 2-4, 2004. The Atoll Research Bulletin, No. 543, Washington, D.C.

DLNR. 2005. Northwestern Hawaiian Islands Marine Refuge. Department of Land and Natural Resources (DLNR). Hawaii Administration Rules, Title 13, Ch. 60.5. State of Hawaii, Honolulu, HI.

Douvere, F. 2008. The importance of marine spatial planning in advancing ecosystem-based sea use management. Marine Policy 32:762-771.

Douvere, F., and C. Ehler. 2008. The role of marine spatial planning in implementing ecosystem-based, sea use management. Marine Policy 32:759-844.

Ecological Applications 1998. Ecosystem management for sustainable fisheries, Ecological Applications 8(1), Supplement.

Ecological Applications 2003. The science of marine reserves. Ecological Applications 13(1), Supplement.

Ecosystem Principles Advisory Panel. 1999. Ecosystem-based fishery management. A report to Congress by the Ecosystem Principles Advisory Panel, as mandated by the Sustainable Fisheries Act amendments to the Magnuson-Stevens Fishery Conservation and Management Act 1996. U.S. Department of Commerce, National Oceanic and Atmospheric Administration, National Marine Fisheries Service, Washington, D.C.

Ehler, C. N., and F. Douvere. 2007. Visions for a sea change. Report of the first international workshop on marine spatial planning. Intergovernmental oceanographic commission and man and the biosphere programme. IOC manual and guides no. 48. IOCAM Dossier no. 4. UNESCO, Paris.

Epstein, P. R., T. E. Ford, C. Puccia, and C. D. A. Possas. 1994. Marine ecosystem health implications for public health. Annals of the New York Academy of Sciences 740:13-23.

Executive Order 199A. Placing Midway Atoll under control of the U.S. Navy. 1903, Washington, D.C.

Executive Order 1019. Establishing the Hawaiian Islands Reservation. February 3, 1909, Washington, D.C.

Executive Order 13178. Northwestern Hawaiian Islands coral reef ecosystem reserve. 65 Fed. Reg. 76903-76910, December 4, 2000, Washington, D.C.

Executive Order 13196. Final Northwestern Hawaiian Islands coral reef ecosystem reserve. 66 Fed. Reg. 7395-7397, January 18, 2001, Washington, D.C.

FAO. 2003. Fisheries management - 2. The ecosystem approach to fisheries. Food and Agricultural Organization of the United Nations (FAO), Rome.

FAO. 2007. Draft International Guidelines on the Management of Deep-sea Fisheries in the High Seas. As adopted by the Expert Consultation on International Guidelines on the Management of Deep-sea Fisheries in the High Seas (Bangkok, Thailand, 11-14 September 2007). Food and Agricultural Organization (FAO) of the United Nations, Bangkok, Thailand.

Fernandes, L., J. O. N. Day, A. Lewis, S. Slegers, B. Kerrigan, D. A. N. Breen, D. Cameron, B. Jago, J. Hall, D. Lowe, J. Innes, J. Tanzer, V. Chadwick, L. Thompson, K. Gorman, M. Simmons, B. Barnett, K. Sampson, G. De'Ath, B. Mapstone, H. Marsh, H. Possingham, I. A. N. Ball, T. Ward, K. Dobbs, J. Aumend, D. E. B. Slater, and K. Stapleton. 2005. Establishing representative no-take areas in the Great Barrier Reef: Large-scale implementation of theory on marine protected areas. Conservation Biology 19:1733-1744.

Folke, C., L. Pritchard Jr, F. Berkes, J. Colding, and U. Svedin. 2007. The problem of fit between ecosystems and institutions: ten years later. Ecology and Society 12:30.

Friedlander, A. M., E. K. Brown, and M. E. Monaco. 2007. Coupling ecology and GIS to evaluate efficacy of marine protected areas in Hawaii. Ecological Applications 17:715-730.

Gaichas, S. K. 2008. A context for ecosystem-based fishery management: Developing concepts of ecosystems and sustainability. Marine Policy 32:393-401.

Galaz, V., P. Olsson, T. Hahn, C. Folke, and U. Svedin. 2007. The problem of fit among biophysical systems, environmental and resource regimes, and broader governance systems: insights and emerging challenges. Pages 147-182 in O. R. Young, L. A. King, and H. Schroder, editors. Institutions and environmental change: principal findings, applications and research frontiers. MIT Press, Cambridge, MA.

Garcia, S. M., A. Zerbi, C. Aliaume, T. Do Chi, and G. Lassarre. 2003. The ecosystem approach to fisheries. FAO Fisheries Technical Paper No. 443. Food and Agricultural Organization of the United Nations., Rome.

Garthe, S., and O. Huppop. 2004. Scaling possible adverse effects of marine wind farms on seabirds: developing and applying a vulnerability index. Journal of Applied Ecology 41:724-734.

Grigg, R. W., and R. T. Pfund. 1980. Proceedings of the symposium on status of resource investigations in the northwestern Hawaiian Islands. UNIHI-SEAGRANT-MR-80-04, Honolulu, HI.

Grigg, R. W., J. J. Polovina, A. M. Friedlander, and S. O. Rohmann. 2008. Biology of the coral reefs of the northwestern Hawaiian Islands. Pages 573-594 in B. M. Riegl, and R. E. Dodge, editors. Coral reefs of the USA. Springer, Berlin.

Grigg, R. W., and K. Y. Tanoue. 1984. Proceedings of the second symposium on resource investigations in the northwestern Hawaiian Islands. UNIHI-SEAGRANT-MR-84-01, Honolulu, HI.

Grumbine, R. 1994. What is ecosystem management? Conservation Biology 8:27-38.

Gunderson, L. H., C. S. Holling, and S. S. Light 1995. Barriers and bridges to the renewal of ecosystems and institutions. Columbia University Press, New York.

Gundlach, E. R., and M. Hayes. 1978. Classification of coastal environments in terms of potential vulnerability to oil spill damage. Marine Technology Society Journal 12:18-27.

Halpern, B. S., K. A. Selkoe, F. Micheli, and C. V. Kappel. 2007. Evaluating and ranking the vulnerability of global marine ecosystems to anthropogenic threats. Conservation Biology 21:1301–1315.

Halpern, B. S., S. Walbridge, K. A. Selkoe, C. V. Kappel, F. Micheli, C. D'Agrosa, J. F. Bruno, K. S. Casey, C. Ebert, H. E. Fox, R. Fujita, D. Heinemann, H. S. Lenihan, E. M. P. Madin, M. T. Perry, E. R. Selig, M. Spalding, R. Steneck, and R. Watson. 2008. A global map of human impact on marine ecosystems. Science 319:948-952.

Hiddink, J. G., S. Jennings, and M. J. Kaiser. 2007. Assessing and predicting the relative ecological impacts of disturbance on habitats with different sensitivities. Journal of Applied Ecology 44:405-413.

Hirsch Hadorn, G., H. Hoffmann-Riem, S. Biber-Klemm, W. Grossenbacher-Mansuy, D. Joye, C. Pohl, U. Wiesmann, and E. Zemp, editors. 2008. Handbook of Transdisciplinary Research. Springer, New York, NY.

Hiscock, K., and H. Tyler-Walters. 2006. Assessing the sensitivity of seabed species and biotopes–The marine life information network (MarLIN). Hydrobiologia 555:309-320.

Hughes, T. P., A. H. Baird, D. R. Bellwood, M. Card, S. R. Connolly, C. Folke, R. Grosberg, O. Hoegh-Guldberg, J. B. C. Jackson, J. Kleypas, J. M. Lough, P. Marshall, M. Nystrom, S. R. Palumbi, J. M. Pandolfi, B. Rosen, and J. Roughgarden. 2003. Climate change, human impacts, and the resilience of coral reefs. Science 301:929-933.

Hughes, T. P., L. H. Gunderson, C. Folke, A. H. Baird, D. Bellwood, F. Berkes, B. Crona, A. Helfgott, H. Leslie, J. Norberg, M. Nyström, P. Olsson, H. Österblom, M. Scheffer, H. Schuttenberg, R. S. Steneck, M. Tengö, M. Troell, B. Walker, J. Wilson, and B. Worm. 2007. Adaptive management of the Great Barrier Reef and the Grand Canyon World Heritage areas. Ambio 36:586–592.

Kittinger, J. N. 2008. The legal nexus in U.S. fisheries management: application in the Hawaiian longline fishery litigation. University of Hawai'i Law Review 30:269-293 [online] http://www2.hawaii.edu/~jkitt/Publications.html.

Kittinger, J. N., K. N. Duin, and B. A. Wilcox. 2009. Commercial fishing, conservation and compatibility in the northwestern Hawaiian Islands. Marine Policy 34:208-217.

Lebel, J. 2003. Health: An ecosystem approach. International Development Research Centre, Ottawa, Canada.

Leslie, H., M. Ruckelshaus, I. R. Ball, S. Andelman, and H. P. Possingham. 2003. Using siting algorithms in the design of marine reserve networks. Ecological Applications 13:185-198.

Leslie, H. M., and K. L. McLeod. 2007. Confronting the challenges of implementing marine ecosystem-based management. Frontiers in Ecology and the Environment 5:540-548.

Link, J. S. 2002. What does ecosystem-based fisheries management mean? Fisheries 27:18-21.

Linstone, H. A., and M. Turoff, editors. 2002. The Delphi Method: Techniques and Applications. New Jersey Institute of Technology, Newark, NJ.

Lubchenco, J., S. R. Palumbi, S. D. Gaines, and S. Andelman. 2003. Plugging a hole in the ocean: the emerging science of marine reserves. Ecological Applications 13:3-7.

Margules, C. R., and R. L. Pressey. 2000. Systematic conservation planning. Nature 405:243-253.

McLeod, K. and H. Leslie (eds.). 2009. Ecosystem-Based Management for the Oceans: Resilience Approaches. Island Press, Washington, D.C.

Memorandum of Agreement. 2006. Memorandum of Agreement Among the State of Hawaii Department of Land and Natural Resources, and the U.S. Department of the Interior, U.S. Fish and Wildlife Service, and the U.S. Department of Commerce, National Oceanic and Atmospheric Administration for Promoting Coordinated Management of the Northwestern Hawaiian Islands Marine National Monument. Dec. 8, 2006, Honolulu, HI.

Michel, J., M. O. Hayes, and P. J. Brown. 1978. Application of the oil spill vulnerability index to the shorelines of Lower Cook Inlet, AK. Environmental Geology 1:107-117.

Millenium Ecosystem Assessment 2005. Ecosystems and human well-being: health synthesis: a report of the Millennium Ecosystem Assessment. World Health Organization and Millenium Ecosystems Assessment, Geneva.

Mitchell, R. K., B. R. Agle, and D. J. Wood. 1997. Toward a theory of stakeholder identification and salience: defining the principle of who and what really counts. The Academy of Management Review 22:853-886.

Norse, E. A., and L. B. Crowder, editors. 2005a. Marine conservation biology: the science of maintaining the sea's biodiversity. Island Press, Washington, D.C.

Norse, E. A., and L. B. Crowder. 2005b. Why marine conservation biology? Pages 1-18 in E. A. Norse, and L. B. Crowder, editors. Marine conservation biology: the science of maintaining the sea's biodiversity. Island Press, Washington, D.C.

Noss, R. F., C. Carroll, K. Vance-Borland, and G. Wuerthner. 2002. A multicriteria assessment of the irreplaceability and vulnerability of sites in the greater Yellowstone ecosystem. Conservation Biology 16:895-908.

NRC 1999. Sustaining marine fisheries. Natural Resources Council. Committee on Ecosystem Management for Sustainable Marine Fisheries. National Academies Press, Washington DC.

Nyström, M., and C. Folke. 2001. Spatial resilience of coral reefs. Ecosystems 4:406-417.

Nyström, M., C. Folke, and F. Moberg. 2000. Coral reef disturbance and resilience in a human-dominated environment. Trends in Ecology & Evolution 15:413-417.

Olsson, P., C. Folke, and T. P. Hughes. 2008. Navigating the transition to ecosystem-based management of the Great Barrier Reef, Australia. Proceedings of the National Academy of Sciences 205:9489-9494.

Parenteau, P. A., D. C. Baur, and J. L. Schorr. 2008. Legal authorities for ecosystem based management in U.S. coastal and ocean areas. Pages 597-654 in D. C. Baur, T. Eichenberg, and M. Sutton, editors. Ocean and Coastal Law and Policy. Section of Environment, Energy and Resources, American Bar Association, Chicago.

Pomeroy, R., and F. Douvere. 2008. The engagement of stakeholders in the marine spatial planning process. Marine Policy **32**:816-822.

Possingham, H. P., I. R. Ball and S. Andelman 2000. Mathematical methods for identifying representative reserve networks. In: S. Ferson and M. Burgman (eds) Quantitative methods for conservation biology. Springer-Verlag, New York, pp. 291-305.

Presidential Proclamation 2416. Renaming the Hawaiian Islands Reservation as the Hawaiian Islands National Wildlife Refuge. July 25, 1940.

Presidential Proclamation 8031. Establishment of the Northwestern Hawaiian Islands Marine National Monument. 71 Fed. Reg. 36443, June 26, 2006, Washington, D.C.

Presidential Proclamation 8112. Amending Proclamation 8031 of June 15, 2006, To Read, ''Establishment of the Papahānaumokuākea Marine National Monument''. 72 Fed. Reg. 10031, February 28, 2007, Washington, D.C.

Ruckelshaus, M., T. Klinger, N. Knowlton, and D. P. DeMaster. 2008. Marine ecosystem-based management in practice: Scientific and governance challenges. BioScience 58:53-63.

Saaty, T. L. 1987. Risk—its priority and probability: the analytic hierarchy process. Risk Analysis 7:159-172.

Salafsky, N., R. Margoluis, and K. Redford. 2001. Adaptive management: A tool for conservation practitioners. Biodiversity Support Program, Washington, D.C.

Scott, S. G., and V. R. Lane. 2000. A stakeholder approach to organizational identity. Academy of Management Review 25:43-62.

Selkoe, K. A., B. S. Halpern, C. M. Ebert, E. C. Franklin, E. R. Selig, K. S. Casey, J. Bruno, and R. J. Toonen. 2008a. A map of human impacts to a "pristine" coral reef ecosystem, the Papahānaumokuākea Marine National Monument. Coral Reefs *in review*. [Do not cite without authors' permission: selkoe@nceas.ucsb.edu].

Selkoe, K. A., B. S. Halpern, and R. J. Toonen. 2008b. Evaluating anthropogenic threats to the Northwestern Hawaiian Islands. Aquatic Conservation: Marine and Freshwater Ecosystems [online] http://dx.doi.org/10.1002/aqc.961.

Sherman, K. 1991. The large marine ecosystem concept: Research and management strategy for living marine resources. Ecological Applications 1:349-360.

Sobel, J., and C. Dahlgren 2004. Marine reserves: a guide to science, design, and use. Island Press, Washington, D.C.

Soule, M. E., and B. A. Wilcox 1980. Conservation biology: an evolutionary-ecological perspective. Sinauer, Sunderland, MA.

State of Hawai'i, National Oceanic and Atmospheric Administration, Office of Hawaiian Affairs, and U.S. Fish and Wildlife Service. 2009. Nomination of Papahānaumokuākea Marine National Monument for Inscription on the World Heritage List. Honolulu, Hawai'i. 280 pgs.

USCG. 2008. personal communication.n J. O'Malley, Honolulu, HI.

USFWS, NOAA, and State of Hawaii. 2008. Papahānaumokuākea Marine National Monument. Monument Management Plan. U.S. Fish and Wildlife Service (USFWS), National Oceanic and Atmospheric Administration (NOAA), State of Hawai'i Department of Land and Natural Resources, Honolulu, HI.

Wilson, K., R. L. Pressey, A. Newton, M. Burgman, H. Possingham, and C. Weston. 2005. Measuring and incorporating vulnerability into conservation planning. Environmental Management 35:527-543.

Wilson, K. A., M. F. McBride, M. Bode, and H. P. Possingham. 2006. Prioritizing global conservation efforts. Nature 440:337-340.

Zacharias, M. A., and E. J. Gregr. 2005. Sensitivity and vulnerability in marine environments: An approach to identifying vulnerable marine areas. Conservation Biology 19:86-97.

ONMS CONSERVATION SERIES PUBLICATIONS

To date, the following reports have been published in the Marine Sanctuaries Conservation Series. All publications are available on the Office of National Marine Sanctuaries Web site.

Preliminary Comparison of Natural Versus Model-predicted Recovery of Vessel-generated Seagrass Injuries in Florida Keys National Marine Sanctuary (ONMS-09-03)

A Comparison of Seafloor Habitats and Associated Benthic Fauna in Areas Open and Closed to Bottom Trawling Along the Central California Continental Shelf (ONMS-09-02)

Chemical Contaminants, Pathogen Exposure and General Health Status of Live and Beach-Cast Washington Sea Otters (*Enhydra lutris kenyoni*) (ONMS-09-01)

Caribbean Connectivity: Implications for Marine Protected Area Management (ONMS-08-07)

Knowledge, Attitudes and Perceptions of Management Strategies and Regulations of FKNMS by Commercial Fishers, Dive Operators, and Environmental Group Members: A Baseline Characterization and 10-year Comparison (ONMS-08-06)

First Biennial Ocean Climate Summit: Finding Solutions for San Francisco Bay Area's Coast and Ocean (ONMS-08-05)

A Scientific Forum on the Gulf of Mexico: The Islands in the Stream Concept (NMSP-08-04)

M/V *ELPIS* Coral Reef Restoration Monitoring Report Monitoring Events 2004-2007 Florida Keys National Marine Sanctuary Monroe County, Florida (NMSP-08-03)

CONNECTIVITY Science, People and Policy in the Florida Keys National Marine Sanctuary (NMSP-08-02)

M/V *ALEC OWEN MAITLAND* Coral Reef Restoration Monitoring Report Monitoring Events 2004-2007 Florida Keys National Marine Sanctuary Monroe County, Florida (NMSP-08-01)

Automated, objective texture segmentation of multibeam echosounder data - Seafloor survey and substrate maps from James Island to Ozette Lake, Washington Outer Coast. (NMSP-07-05)

Observations of Deep Coral and Sponge Assemblages in Olympic Coast National Marine Sanctuary, Washington (NMSP-07-04)

A Bioregional Classification of the Continental Shelf of Northeastern North America for Conservation Analysis and Planning Based on Representation (NMSP-07-03)

M/V *WELLWOOD* Coral Reef Restoration Monitoring Report Monitoring Events 2004-2006 Florida Keys National Marine Sanctuary Monroe County, Florida (NMSP-07-02)

Survey report of NOAA Ship McArthur II cruises AR-04-04, AR-05-05 and AR-06-03: Habitat classification of side scan sonar imagery in support of deep-sea coral/sponge explorations at the Olympic Coast National Marine Sanctuary (NMSP-07-01)

2002 - 03 Florida Keys National Marine Sanctuary Science Report: An Ecosystem Report Card After Five Years of Marine Zoning (NMSP-06-12)

Habitat Mapping Effort at the Olympic Coast National Marine Sanctuary - Current Status and Future Needs (NMSP-06-11)

M/V *CONNECTED* Coral Reef Restoration Monitoring Report Monitoring Events 2004-2005 Florida Keys National Marine Sanctuary Monroe County, Florida (NMSP-06-010)

M/V *JACQUELYN L* Coral Reef Restoration Monitoring Report Monitoring Events 2004-2005 Florida Keys National Marine Sanctuary Monroe County, Florida (NMSP-06-09)

M/V *WAVE WALKER* Coral Reef Restoration Baseline Monitoring Report - 2004 Florida Keys National Marine Sanctuary Monroe County, Florida (NMSP-06-08)

Olympic Coast National Marine Sanctuary Habitat Mapping: Survey report and classification of side scan sonar data from surveys HMPR-114-2004-02 and HMPR-116-2005-01 (NMSP-06-07)

A Pilot Study of Hogfish (*Lachnolaimus maximus* Walbaum 1792) Movement in the Conch Reef Research Only Area (Northern Florida Keys) (NMSP-06-06)

Comments on Hydrographic and Topographic LIDAR Acquisition and Merging with Multibeam Sounding Data Acquired in the Olympic Coast National Marine Sanctuary (ONMS-06-05)

Conservation Science in NOAA's National Marine Sanctuaries: Description and Recent Accomplishments (ONMS-06-04)

Normalization and characterization of multibeam backscatter: Koitlah Point to Point of the Arches, Olympic Coast National Marine Sanctuary - Survey HMPR-115-2004-03 (ONMS-06-03)

Developing Alternatives for Optimal Representation of Seafloor Habitats and Associated Communities in Stellwagen Bank National Marine Sanctuary (ONMS-06-02)

Benthic Habitat Mapping in the Olympic Coast National Marine Sanctuary (ONMS-06-01)

Channel Islands Deep Water Monitoring Plan Development Workshop Report (ONMS-05-05)

Movement of yellowtail snapper (Ocyurus chrysurus Block 1790) and black grouper (Mycteroperca bonaci Poey 1860) in the northern Florida Keys National Marine Sanctuary as determined by acoustic telemetry (MSD-05-4)

The Impacts of Coastal Protection Structures in California's Monterey Bay National Marine Sanctuary (MSD-05-3)

An annotated bibliography of diet studies of fish of the southeast United States and Gray's Reef National Marine Sanctuary (MSD-05-2)

Noise Levels and Sources in the Stellwagen Bank National Marine Sanctuary and the St. Lawrence River Estuary (MSD-05-1)

Biogeographic Analysis of the Tortugas Ecological Reserve (MSD-04-1)

A Review of the Ecological Effectiveness of Subtidal Marine Reserves in Central California (MSD-04-2, MSD-04-3)

Pre-Construction Coral Survey of the M/V Wellwood Grounding Site (MSD-03-1)

Olympic Coast National Marine Sanctuary: Proceedings of the 1998 Research Workshop, Seattle, Washington (MSD-01-04)

Workshop on Marine Mammal Research & Monitoring in the National Marine Sanctuaries (MSD-01-03)

A Review of Marine Zones in the Monterey Bay National Marine Sanctuary (MSD-01-2)

Distribution and Sighting Frequency of Reef Fishes in the Florida Keys National Marine Sanctuary (MSD-01-1)

Flower Garden Banks National Marine Sanctuary: A Rapid Assessment of Coral, Fish, and Algae Using the AGRRA Protocol (MSD-00-3)

The Economic Contribution of Whalewatching to Regional Economies: Perspectives From Two National Marine Sanctuaries (MSD-00-2)

Olympic Coast National Marine Sanctuary Area to be Avoided Education and Monitoring Program (MSD-00-1)

Multi-species and Multi-interest Management: an Ecosystem Approach to Market Squid (*Loligo opalescens*) Harvest in California (MSD-99-1)